Sugar & Honey

VANESSA M. WHITE

I0086409

Published By:
Jasher Press & Co.
www.jasherpress.com
P.O. Box 14520
New Bern, NC 28561

Copyright© 2011
Interior Text Design by Pamela S. Almore
Cover Design by Justin D. White

ISBN: 978-0615554112
Vanessa M. White

First Edition
Printed and bound in the United States of America
Copyright © 2011

Sugar & Honey

Vanessa M. White

JASHER PRESS & CO.

DEDICATION
To the parents and guardians of children all over the world.

ACKNOWLEDGEMENTS

A special thanks to the late Reverend Arthur A. Colson Sr., who taught me to seek the truth.

Reverend Vianna Witcher-Jones for always reminding me, "Nessa, you can do it."

Apostle Anna P. Fulcher for saying Holiness is always right.

Deacon Bobby McClain, who has often told me, "Vanessa, don't give up."

Mrs. Marian Mc Clain (retired Librarian), who was the first to encourage me to write.

CONTENTS

Introduction

This book is not Parenting Skills class 101. It's mostly my observations of parenting trends today. It's intended to open parents' eyes and show them how the Lord God wants them to treat children. God gave them children in the first place. Naturally, it is He who has the right to show them how to care for His little ones. He wrote the manual. Even before the world began, He had a plan for each person's life. (Ephesians 1:3-4) Parents have the right, as well as the responsibility, to connect with God to find out how to rear His children. (Judges 13:6-8)

God revealed His way for childrearing to me in a dream. One night, I had a terrible dream. I dreamed that a big black snake was chasing after the children. It bit them, and they fell dead. I ran to the tool shed, got a garden ho, and began killing the snake. In the dream, my aunt asked me what I was doing. I told her that if parents don't get themselves together and get saved, their children will die. After some interpretation, I realized that the dream was my confirmation that God has given me the right and the responsibility to speak out and fight for the souls of the children. I have authorization to say what God told me to say to help the children.

Children Are A Gift From God

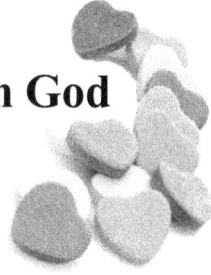

C hildren have been given to parents as a gift from God. He sent them to this earth to be developed into the image of Jesus Christ. Once they've been transformed into the image of Christ, they are fit to live in the presence of God for all eternity. Parents have a duty to teach and train these children in the ways of the Lord so that when they come of age, they can call on the Lord and be saved. I have observed parents who mold a child into their own image instead of the image of Christ. Those parents have usurped God's position. The child belongs to the Lord, who has only given him to the parent for a season. Children are a gift from God.

God gave man the ability to reproduce children. God created men's and women's anatomic designs so that reproduction is possible. Marriage, the only vehicle instituted and approved by God, gives people permission to use their bodies for reproduction. Having children out of wedlock is a total act of rebellion against God. It's like stealing the power to produce life.

Will a man rob God? (Malachi 3:8) Beyond a shadow of a doubt, the answer is yes. Having sexual

11

intercourse outside of wedlock or using artificial means of fertilization to have a baby is stealing—yet Christians and non-Christians do it every day. They do not have the permission to be fruitful and multiply. (Genesis 1:27-28)

Man has the knowledge to create an atomic bomb—but he does not have permission from God to use it to destroy human lives. Man has the knowledge to create test-tube babies, artificial insemination, and cloning—but he does not have permission from God to use it. What gives man the right to steal or try to improve what God has already created? God set the plan in order before the world began. What gives man the right to try to open a womb that God has closed? If a couple cannot produce a baby, they should go to God, humble themselves, and ask for His mercy and grace. Maybe then He will relent and open the womb. If He chooses not to, then the couple getting a baby "by hook or by crook" is being disrespectful to God.

Children are a gift. Going to your neighbor's house without permission and picking apples off his tree is stealing. Going to your neighbor's house and picking the apples that have fallen from the tree is also stealing. Thieves and robbers will not enter the Kingdom of God (I Corinthians 6:10-11), nor will any parent who has taken a child without God's permission. Remember—thou shalt not steal. (Exodus 20:15)

Sacrificing the Children

How many parents have their children christened or offered up to the Lord? How many offer these children up for blessings and protection? I've seen countless parents try to make their children smaller versions of themselves. I've seen parents lose their children, or the child dies because they stole him from the Lord. How many parents have you seen crying and screaming out to God at a funeral? They didn't ask for the Lord's blessings on that child while he was alive. When something tragic happens, they cry and moan, "Oh, Lord! Oh, Lord! Why did you take my child? He was so young. Why didn't you take me instead?"

Ananias and Sapphire lost their lives for lying and stealing the thing that they had already dedicated to God. (Acts 5:1-11) Once a child is offered to the Lord, what makes parents think that they have the right to take the child back? Who do they think they're playing with? God is for real. He is omnipotent and almighty. (Genesis 20:1-6) What parents don't realize is that by not offering the child to God, they have given him over to Satan by default. They are sacrificing their children for destruction. Ezekiel the priest gave warning to the Israelite people about sacrificing their children to pagan gods. (Ezekiel 16:20-23) These helpless children were given over to idol worship instead of worship of the true and living God Jehovah.

Parents then and now have forgotten that their children are blessings sent from God. The pagan gods of today are money and financial gain. In order to "get a leg up" in the financial world or to have more material wealth, parents place their children in institutions like daycare, military schools, and boarding schools. They send their children to other people who teach them the ways of the world instead of the ways of God. The child's home training, nurturing, and religious education should be the parents' responsibility. Instead, the God of Mammon is being thoroughly worshipped and highly favored. (Matthew 6:24) The children are being sacrificed to the powers of darkness. Satan and all of his demons are getting an early chance at a child's soul. Evil starts killing the child's spirit from birth.

Both saved and unsaved parents are throwing their children into the sacrificial fires of hell. They don't realize that Jesus loves the little children. He has a book of remembrance of what people do to little children. (Revelation 20:12) Unless they repent, parents who throw their children into the worldly sacrificial fires will themselves be thrown into the lake of fire that burns forever and ever. This eternal fire can never be quenched. Parents need to wake up and save themselves and their children. Run to Jesus, and He will save you.

Spiritual Attacks

There was a war in Heaven. (Revelation 12:7) Satan and one third of the heavenly host who followed him were kicked out. Banished to the earth with him were the angels we now call demons. Adam and Eve listened to Satan and were thus kicked out of the Garden of Eden. The loss of their comfy, cozy homes was the punishment for all those rebellious earthly and heavenly beings. Like the proverbial rock being thrown into the lake, the ripple effect magnified into so great a proportion that all the future seed born of Adam and Eve were punished.

The Lord God hates all sin and disobedience. He tells us this in His written Word—the Holy Bible. Satan is a liar. He is the father of all lies. Have you ever heard the lie spread by Satan that babies never sin? They haven't been in the world long enough to learn how to sin. They are born innocent so that when they die, they will go straight to Heaven. Being paraphrased, the Psalmist in 51:5 says, "Surely I was sinful at birth, sinful from the time my mother conceived me." The Psalmist knows that children are born in sin and shaped in inequity.

Some parents have been hoodwinked into thinking that their child is greater than the Son of God, who never sinned. Because some parents hold this belief, Satan convinces them not to pray for their children's souls and not to teach or train them in the ways of the Lord. Some Christian parents have been deceived into thinking that their children are innocent of sin. They will swear to you that their child never sins. In reality, children tell lies, cheat, steal, fight, and even murder their own parents.

In Romans 3:23, the Apostle Paul reminds us that all of mankind has sinned. This includes children. If God didn't let the holy angels get away with sin, how do parents think that their little sugar and honey or sweet peas will escape his wrath? Satan doesn't want any of Adam's seed returning to the comfy, cozy heavenly home that he was kicked out of. He has declared war on mankind and uses every tactic possible to prevent this from happening.

For instance, Satan attacks children while they are still in the womb. He leads the parents to engage in risky behaviors before, during, and after the conception of the child. Some of these behaviors are alcohol abuse, drug abuse (legal or illegal), smoking, extreme emotional stress or trauma, sexual acts that cause diseases, or dabbling in the occult or black magic. There are many tricks Satan uses to destroy the child.

The Bible says that life is in the blood. (Leviticus 17:14) Unborn fetuses receive every bit of what's being transferred from the placenta into their bloodstreams. Not only are they being poisoned to death by what their mothers consume or ingest—their own fathers are just as responsible. Any illegal chemicals or diseases the father has in his body travel in his sperm and fertilize the egg. From the moment of conception, the poor child doesn't have a chance to come out whole and healthy.

Where is the parents' love for their child? Where is

the appreciation for the gift of life that the Lord God has bestowed upon the parents? It's like God has given someone a special gift. The person opens it, relieves his bowels in it, closes it, and accuses God of giving him a filthy gift. How awful to accuse the Lord God of such a deed! It's not in the Lord's nature to give a filthy gift. That person ruined his own gift when he yielded his mind, body, and soul to the devil and passed along a defective seed. When the baby comes out physically deformed and mentally or emotionally ill, the parents want to blame God. They say that God made a mistake.

How many times does the Lord have to take the bum rap for man's wicked, evil behavior? Satan has parents so blinded that they don't recognize that it is *he* who leads them to destroy their own children. Our adversary knows that his time is short, and in the end, he'll be thrown into the lake of fire and brimstone that burns forever and ever. He wants every soul that is born on this earth to burn with him.

When Jesus was born, Satan used King Herod to try to kill our sweet little baby. Matthew 2:13-21 tells us how God protected Jesus so that when the time was fulfilled, mankind could be redeemed and return to spend eternity in God's glory. Children have souls. Parents are responsible for the child's soul until he reaches the age of knowledge and responsibility.

A line in the popular children's bedtime prayer goes like this: "If I should die before I wake, I pray the Lord my soul to take." Isn't it amazing how some parents leave it up to the child to ask the Lord to keep their souls safe while they sleep? The adversary doesn't sleep. He is out there day and night trying to destroy the children. Parents, whether they are Christian or not, must open their eyes and realize the seriousness of the spiritual war going on out there for their children's souls. If parents love their children, they wouldn't leave it up to the child to ask for safe passage into the heavenly Kingdom.

It's true that God hears the prayers of a little child—but how many children fall asleep before bedtime? Those children can't pray and ask for anything, because they've fallen asleep in their car seats, on the living room floor, at the kitchen table, on the sofa, on a piece of playground equipment—and some in the bathtub. Once they connect with Jesus Christ, parents have the power to fight off spiritual attacks and win the battle for their children's souls.

Joy and Laughter

There's something refreshing about the laughter of a child. Hearing them laugh somehow lifts your spirits. But some children never laugh because they're being abused. Whether it is physical, mental, emotional, or sexual, the wounds of abuse hurt the soul as well as the spirit. Laughter is a gift from God. When parents don't take good care of or protect their children, laughter dies out. If laughter is supposed to be good medicine, why do these children have to be sick? (Proverbs 15:13, 17:22) Why can't their healing come forth? Why is God's medicine not good enough for these little ones?

Parents are allowing Satan to rob their offspring of joy and laughter. In Nehemiah 8:10, the prophet says, "The joy of the Lord is your strength." Parents should realize that children have no strength of their own to fight the wiles of the devil. They cannot do it alone. That's one reason why some of them are so full of hatred and violence and use guns to kill themselves and other children. They want to fight, but the power of Satan is so strong that they fight the wrong people. These children are full of the demons that hide in the darkness of the soul, where only the light of Christ can enter and set them free.

Children are dying every day because their souls are in blackness, where no laughter can enter or escape. Parents need to grab hold of the joy and laughter of Christ. They should set the example so their children will see it and learn to be free. For God's sake—let the children laugh.

Selfish Parents

You and your children will be cursed. (Jeremiah 29:32) When parents rebel against the Lord, they bring curses upon themselves and their children. Their selfishness will cause a seal of destruction to fall upon the child's head. Not only are curses handed down to children, but junk from the parents' past lives is passed down, too. Unsaved parents don't realize that they're causing their own sins to be handed down from generation to generation. Christian parents should already know not to do that. Yet some Christian parents can't help themselves because they're still just as immature as they can be. They're so obsessed with their own lives that they don't have time to teach their children right from wrong. These parents are spiritually undeveloped. The writer in Hebrews 5:12-14 talks about how these people are still drinking milk instead of eating the meat of God's Word.

Some parents are so selfish that they have forgotten about their young. Their children are lost. They treat them as if they don't exist. They act like the children have no feelings or emotions. On the contrary—children are packed with so many contrasting feelings and emotions that they need someone to explain the reality of what's going on. They must be taught how to identify the feelings that rule their bodies and minds. By their teenage years, children experience hardly anything but emotions running wild. Jesus loves the little children and wants them to grow up being taught in a godly manner.

Parents should stop putting kids down and acting like they're pint-sized adults—they're not adults yet. Parents should stop expecting them to be mature beyond their age or abilities. Fruit on trees doesn't ripen overnight, and neither do children. Let them have their season of growth. Satan has deceived some parents' minds so badly that he has them thinking that children can "fend for themselves"—in other words, make it on their own. Some children have had to assume the role of an adult or a parent. The child is pushed into a role that was never designed for him to be in. He never had a chance to be a child first.

A good example of a child working and living in adulthood before he could finish his childhood is the late singer Michael Jackson. Some children have to be the breadwinner and the responsible one in the family. When one parent has left the family for various reasons, children have been made to act in the role of the other parent. They fill in the gap by being the man or woman of the house. That's one of the reasons why some adults today are lying on psychiatric couches, crying their hearts out because they never got a chance to play and actually act like a child. Having to be the man or woman of the house traumatized them. Some parents hate or resent their child for being born. They say the child is messing up their lives, so they send him off to boarding school or some military academy. Or, worse yet, they conduct their lives so badly that the child becomes a ward of the state to be placed in some foster home.

These selfish parents make all kinds of excuses for not loving and taking proper care of their children. Their hatred and ignorance is so strong that they leave their children out there for the forces of spiritual darkness to attack them. The evil in the parents' hearts causes them to say, "I never wanted children anyway." What they fail to realize is that when they get saved and love the Lord, this love will spill over to their children, too.

Death Sentence

Children are dying every day—and parents are the ones killing them. With their mouths, they say that they love their kids. But with their actions, they destroy the child's life before it begins. If parents don't get themselves together, their children will die. Sin is sin. The wages of sin is death. The child is under a death sentence from the time he comes out of the womb until he personally chooses salvation and rebirth through Jesus Christ. The worldly parents are already dead in trespasses and sin. They and their children are on the road to judgment.

Christian parents who aren't following the Lord are on the wrong path, too. They are in error because they're not walking in obedience to God's ways. They set an example of dead works, dead beliefs, and dead faith. These lukewarm Christians are blind to how their lives affect their children. They need to wake up and see that they haven't been teaching God's Word to their children. They haven't been praying for life to flow into their child's soul. They're playing right into Satan's hands to destroy God's little seedlings. Children don't stand a chance. Even men on death row can appeal their sentences. They want mercy to continue living life. Children have no say-so or appellate rights. They're going to die unless their parents lift them up to the Lord God for mercy and blessings.

Parents have the power to save children by bringing them to Jesus. The Lord Jesus said, "The thief cometh not but for to steal, and kill, and to destroy. I am come that they might have life, and have it more abundantly." (John 10:10) Whose fault is it when a child dies? Whose fault is it when one of those precious souls leaves the earth? Do we blame the parents, the child, or God? Do we blame the devil because he's sworn to kill the woman's seed? The dragon was waiting to devour the child as soon as it was born. (Revelation 12:1-5)

Parents are handing their children over to Satan every day. The ones that aren't doing this think that they can fight the powers of darkness all by themselves to save their children. They're deceived into believing that they don't need to call on the Lord to help them raise that child to be a mighty person of God. When the parents fail to protect their children from the evil of this world, the Lord sometimes steps in and sends His angels to move the child to safety. These angels come in the form of pastors, social workers, child protective agencies, law enforcement officials, doctors, judges, family members, neighbors, and friends of the family. These people have been given power to watch over and protect children.

Adam and Eve's sin brought death and damnation to the world. Through His sacrificial death and resurrection, Jesus Christ brought us back to life in God. We can now have a part in the Kingdom because of what Christ did for us. If no one protects the children or teaches them how to get to Christ, their lives will remain in sin and degradation. They'll die in their sins and never be connected to Christ. Neither children nor adults can keep themselves alive because the wages of sin is death. If the parents have allowed anyone to hurt their child or prevent him from coming to Christ, their penalty will be great.

In this world, there's no escaping getting paid for the wages of sin, which is death. But thank God that Jesus Christ stepped out of eternity, came into this world, and died for our children and us. He took the payment for our sins by hanging on the cross.

Till Death Do Us Part

"May he rest in peace" is a popular saying when a person dies. "Till death do us part" is a common vow made between married people. However, some parents will not let go of their child, even in death. A poltergeist is a childlike spirit who has died but hasn't gone to the other side yet. It's a spirit who's trapped between two worlds and cannot rest. When these spirits are in a house, their childish acts or pranks are ways that they're trying to communicate. Being in a spiritual realm and trying to talk to people in a natural realm just doesn't work.

Children in the natural world don't know how to express themselves properly, either. They have feelings, but they don't know how to explain them. They act out different behaviors, trying to show how they feel. Sometimes parents don't understand that the child (living or dead) is just trying to communicate. Whether parents are the ones who refuse to let the dead child cross over or whether it's the child refusing to leave because he's worried about his parents, that soul is trapped.

Some parents who claim that they love their children build shrines for them. For example, they'll keep the child's bedroom just like it was before he died. They display little mementos or place favorite objects all over the room that belonged to the child. They won't rearrange the furniture or change a single thing in the room, thus trapping that person's spirit in the house. No wonder the poltergeist spirits are angry and tear things up or throw things around the room. They need to leave the natural realm of life. The child is held in limbo on this side of the grave by parents who love him too much.

Isn't it amazing how the power of love is so great that it can be used to keep a soul from traveling on its journey from death to the next world? Have you ever noticed how people who are terminally ill will keep holding on because of someone's love? They're in pain, tired of the prolonged sickness, and ready to leave this world—but their loved ones won't let them go. The sick person will hang on and endure suffering for the sake of his beloved. When the loved ones finally come to peace or resignation that the sick person is dying, they then give permission for him to leave. The sick person lets go and dies quickly thereafter.

Parents who say that they will never do anything to hurt their child are lying. They hurt their child by holding onto his spirit long after death has come to claim the body. Those parents are fighting against God and the natural order of things. They're in rebellion against the true and living God. They put up a fight to keep that child with them. They say, "God, you're not going to get my child back. I'm angry with you for taking him away from me, and I won't serve you. I don't want your son Jesus Christ to be Lord over my life. Therefore, I'm not going to serve him, either." These parents place their children so high on a pedestal that there is no room for the real God. There's a problem with that. Matthew 10:37 says that those parents aren't worthy because they put their son or daughter before

Christ. Their children belong to God, and they're not little gods themselves. (Matthew 4:9-10) What some parents have is not love, but idolatry. Satan has entered their hearts. They're full of disobedience against God.

Some parents live vicariously through their children. If their child is a god, that makes them one, too. If the child dies, they justify their actions by saying that God put love in the universe, and they have a right to use the power of love against the Creator. They actually try to fight God by holding onto the child's spirit. They use what King Solomon said about love being as strong as death as their weapon. (Solomon 8:6)

The first few verses of the Ten Commandments tell us to have no other gods. (Exodus 20:1-5) Who do these parents think they are when they try to come up against the Almighty? Man has no control over his own life. (James 4:14-17) In 1 Corinthians 6:20, the angels ask, "What is man that thou are mindful of him?" Isaiah 43:7 tells me that man was created for God's pleasure. How can the dust of the earth fight and win anything? (Genesis 2:7) God is Alpha and Omega. (Revelation 1:8) The devil raised himself up against God and lost.

Hardheaded, stiff-necked, rebellious parents who try to hold onto their children and keep them from resting in peace will not win. All that awaits those parents is the lake of fire that burns forever and ever.

Sex and Sexuality

S atan is the God of this world. Christians are warned not to love the world or lust after the things in it. 1 John 2:15-17 tells us that the only thing in the world is the lust of the flesh, the lust of the eyes, and the pride of life. Our fore parents Adam and Eve were victims of all these lusts. Eve saw the fruit good to eat (lust of the flesh). She saw that it pleased the eyes (lust of the eyes). It could make her wise (pride of life). (Genesis 3:3-7) When she and Adam ate the forbidden fruit, their lusts were satisfied, and their action set all creation in a downward spiral.

Lust and evil desire are dangerous things. Ever since the Garden of Eden incident, man has been tempted by the sin of lust. The lust of the flesh and man's carnal desires are so great that we use sex to merchandise everything from toothpaste to toilet paper. Sex sells. There are hardly any products advertised that don't have some form of sexual innuendo attached to them. We know that God created sex, and everything He made was declared good. Everything He created is good in its proper place. The Lord has a plan for the sexuality of every man, woman, and child on this earth. He set the standards for how people

33

should conduct themselves sexually.

Satan has deceived people into rebelling against God's plan. He leads people full of lust to commit rape, incest, fornication, and all kinds of sexually abusive acts against each other. Their sin is so great that they commit these acts on little children, too. Because children can't defend themselves properly, the people who commit these acts think that they're getting away with something. What they don't realize is that their souls stand in the balance. Judgment awaits them in the end.

Unsaved parents are clueless because they're blinded by their own lust. They follow Satan's destructive plan. He is like a roaring lion, out seeking whom he may devour. (1 Peter 5:8) Christian parents had better wake up and teach their children God's holy standards for sexual relationships. All of our moral and immoral choices have long-term effects. Immoral acts affect our children because they can be passed down from generation to generation. Children are destroyed for lack of knowledge of God's standards. God puts sex glands in a child while he is still being formed in his mother's womb. He predetermines the time and circumstances under which the sex glands grow and are to be used. The sex hormones are made to grow and develop as the child grows. All aspects and conditions of life are predetermined by the Lord. (Ecclesiastes 3:1-15)

Watch little children. They'll play with their vaginas or penises anywhere they choose, public or private. They can feel the sexual and hormonal changes in their bodies even if they can't understand what's happening to them. All they know is that it feels good. While these children are going through their normal growth patterns, Satan comes and attacks them with evil spirits of lust and other sexual demons. These demons propel children into an arena of sex that they're not physically, mentally, or spiritually ready for. Like bad fruit, children are cast off out of season. Sex hormones are activated before the proper time, and children are left wide open for destruction.

Sexually promiscuous children are under the demonic power of lust. Instead of being exploited, they need to be protected.

Unsaved parents need to get saved and do spiritual warfare for their children. Christian parents need to stand in the gap for their children. As the child grows, it is the parents' responsibility to teach him God's standards for sexual behavior.

Like Father, Like Son

O ne way to kill the beast is to write the story. I write this story so that the children will live. It is my mission in life to write this book. The greatest story ever told is the one where our Father which art in Heaven loved His children so much that He sacrificed His son Jesus to bring us back in fellowship with Himself.

Parents want their children to be just like them. They want their sons and daughters to be a chip off the old block—to follow in their footsteps and be a miniature version of themselves. It's no different with God. He sent his son Jesus to be the example for us on how to live, please, and be a child of God. In John 14:8-14, the disciple Phillip wanted Jesus to show him and the other disciples the Father. Jesus had to explain to them that when they were looking at Him, they were looking at the Father.

Jesus came to give eternal life to God's children, whereas unrighteous parents can only give sin and iniquity to their children. They teach them how to lie, cheat, steal, fornicate, and take the Lord's name in vain. They also teach them the world's view that "life just doesn't get any better than this." All the unsaved parents know is the world—so they poison the child's mind with the philosophy of the world.

On the other hand, Christian parents want their children to be like them, too. What some of them don't realize is that they aren't perfect and they live in a fallen world. They need to teach their children to be like Jesus. Taking on the likeness of Christ is of the utmost importance. They fail to stress the point of having Jesus in your heart and mind. In the book of Kings 2:2-4, David charged his son Solomon to walk in God's ways and to keep His commandments.

Some parents fail to deny themselves, pick up their crosses, and follow the Lord. They need to deny the urge to pattern a child after themselves. They need to pick up their cross of suffering—parenthood—and follow Jesus.

I never said that this would be easy. Parenting is never easy, so please don't kill the messenger. Don't throw this book in the trash yet. Keep reading it until the end, or at least until you feel you've gotten your money's worth.

Parents are the portals by which children come into the world. They are responsible for their children's souls until those children reach the age of accountability. Being a parent and being a Christian does not equal being perfect. Sometimes the best of intentions fail. Sometimes sin gets in the way of the parent's ability to set a good example for their child. But thank God for His mercy and forgiveness of sin. The Lord knows our frailties and loves us anyway. Will parents love their children enough to plant the seeds of life in them? Will they allow the Lord Jesus to bring forth the harvest of the soul? I sincerely hope and pray so.

Religious Abuse

If parents are not saved and don't know the Lord, how will their children know to seek the Lord? Some parents send their children to church, yet they don't go themselves. The message being given is that children have to go to church, whereas adults can stay home. In reality, the child looks at what the parents do and not what they say. Going to church alone places him in a religious environment, but there is no parental presence to model Christian values or behavior. The child is being taught the words of God in church with no one at home to display how to put those words into action.

Oftentimes, when the child grows up, he becomes angry with his parents for making him go to church all the time. Now that he's an adult, he rationalizes that if church wasn't good enough for his parents, it's not good enough for him, either. He justifies his behavior by saying that his parents didn't go to church; therefore, it's not important enough for him and his children to go. Do you blame the child who is now an adult, or do you blame his parents for neglecting proper religious education? Do you blame the parents for pushing the child away from God? Do you blame the parents for the grandchildren not having a chance to learn of the Savior? How many generations will not be taught to love and seek the Lord?

The popular world belief is that when parents send their children to church, they themselves don't have to go because they have performed their religious duty. The popular Christian belief is that the entire family goes to church, learns of God, and serves Him. (Joshua 24:15)

Teach Your Children

If the parents' lifestyle of rebellion against God has spilled over and caused one of their little ones to miss out on salvation and the sweet communion of the Holy Spirit, then woe be unto those parents. (Matthew 18:5-7, Psalms 129:1-8) Who will mourn for these children like Rachel did in Jeremiah 31:15? If a saved or unsaved parent is the cause of the child's soul being lost, then the penalty will be so high that it will be humanly impossible to pay. Only through Jesus Christ can that debt be paid. I personally would hate to fall into the hands of an angry God.

The wisest thing to do is to repent and get saved if you're not already. If you already belong to Christ, then repent and rededicate your life to Him. The next thing is to teach your children. Teach them about the ways of the Lord. (Psalms 78:1-7) You must talk to them about God's words wherever you go. (Deuteronomy 6:1-9) Love the Lord God with all your heart, soul, and mind. Practice a holy lifestyle so that the children and the whole world may see it and emulate it. Your reward will be great now and in the world to come. Lastly, pray for and bless your children's lives—then pray some more. Never cease to pray.

Parents Don't Get It

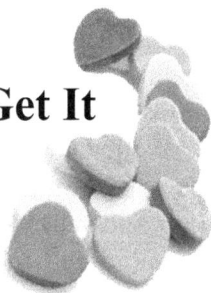

Some Christian parents don't get it. For various reasons, they won't go to the Lord and allow Him to heal those unresolved issues in their lives that keep them stuck spiritually. They're so focused on their own hurt and pain that they're not watching out for the children. How can they give glory to the Lord when the hurt and pain has been imbedded so deeply in their hearts and souls that they don't trust Jesus to scoop it out? (1 Chronicles 16:29) Satan's seeds of doubt and mistrust are planted to confuse the mind into not believing the Almighty God who spoke the universe into existence. Parents don't believe that God can speak to a situation and make everything alright. Knowingly or unknowingly, these parents have passed down the pain and sorrow to the very children whom they say they love.

Children who have this happen to them don't stand a chance. They have no say- so about what they inherit from their parents. The burden of sin they receive is too heavy. The child learns to absorb the heavy burden and takes on the parents' emotional baggage. When he becomes an adult, the child not only carries around his own baggage, but his parents' leftover stuff, too. God didn't mean for things like this to happen. Some children are never able to live their own lives. They're trapped in their parents' lives, and they wind up carrying the parents' burdens to their own graves. These children are the super-responsible ones. The roles are reversed. They're the ones who end up taking care of their parents' emotional hurts instead of the other way around. They kiss the proverbial boo-boo and make the parents feel better. These children are so enmeshed in their parents' lives that the invisible umbilical cord never gets cut.

I've often heard this saying: "That child acts just like his mother or father." That saying is tragic and sometimes so true. If the parents don't ask the Lord for forgiveness and restoration, their inequity will surely be passed to the next generation. With no power to fight back or help themselves, children don't realize what's happening to them. Instead of using their children as dumping grounds for life's troubles, parents need to call on God's son, Jesus Christ—the only child who's ever been able to help anyone. Their natural children were never meant to bring them pain relief. Flesh and blood cannot save you. It is, was, and always will be our Lord Jesus Christ who brings the saving grace. Forgiveness, healing, and restoration are available for the taking. Go to God's child—not your own child—with your burdens, and leave them to Him.

I'm Late

Some saved and unsaved parents who have special jobs to do tend to neglect their children. They work as the head of some big corporation, the pastor of a church, a commanding officer in a military division, a doctor, a lawyer, or even a high school football coach. These people are not only responsible to fulfill the duties of their jobs, but also to train the child in the way he should go. (Proverbs 22:6)

Some parents totally forget about their children. They hide their heads in a hole like an ostrich and pretend like the kids don't exist. They see a child who shows signs of being an independent thinker, so they reason with themselves that the child doesn't need anything. They think that the child can make it on his own. They don't spend time with the child or even talk to him. They're so busy with their own lives and jobs that the child's little problems and little world are of no significance to them. Since they spend little or no time with the child, there is no bond built between them. The child becomes nothing and is unimportant to the parents. The child grows up thinking that his parents never loved him. Unless someone steps in, the child never really learns to show love.

People often say to a person that his father or mother was a great person. They ask how it is that that person turned out to be the opposite. Do they ever think that maybe the person is the way he is because his parents never spent any time with him? He was never trained in the way of righteousness, love, honor, or respect.

The old saying that you can't get blood out of a turnip is so true. Parents' being so busy, whether for God or a selfish purpose, brings a curse on the heads of their children. Parents who continually neglect their children don't really love their children. Even Moses got into trouble with God for neglecting his son. (Exodus 4:18-26) He was so busy dealing with Pharaoh that he couldn't be bothered with his own son.

In the Old Testament days, King Solomon said that there is nothing new under the sun. In our world today, it's the same way. Parents are still neglecting their children. Malachi 4:5-6 tells us how God is displeased with this neglecting of children and has taken steps to remedy it.

Things That Go Bump In The Night

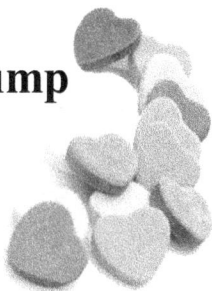

One night, I had a dream in which I changed my baby's diaper and put him to bed. Later on, I put my pajamas on and settled into bed. For some reason, I woke up. I was about to check on the baby when I saw this dark figure overshadowing me, trying to pull me off the bed. Seeing that it was an evil spirit, I rebuked it in the name of Jesus. It stopped pulling me and grabbed my son. I snatched my son back from the demon's hands and physically fought with it. I was yelling at it, pleading the blood of Jesus and rebuking it in the name of Jesus. When I woke up from the dream, I heard myself yelling and screaming at the demon. "You won't get my son! You won't get my son!"

After lying in bed for awhile, I realized what had happened. I was fighting for my child's soul. Demons attack and possess our children. Have you ever heard people say that a child is evil or has a bad spirit in him? Parents have to constantly look out for their children's souls. Christian parents who have been born again have the eyes of their understanding opened to the spiritual world. They live, walk, and breathe in the natural as well as the spiritual realm. Worldly or unsaved parents cannot see into this realm.

Christian parents have no excuse for being blindsided by the evil that comes from the darkness. John 3:4-5 says that in Jesus there is light, and this light shines so you can see all things. It's a terrible thing to love darkness, remain in darkness, and allow the evil beings to overtake your child's soul. (John 3:19-21) Children are weak and vulnerable. They live under a cloud of ignorance to God's ways. Until they grow up, get saved, and are born again, they remain separated from the wisdom of God. However, Christian parents are given the power and the right of authority to fight for the souls of their offspring. Even a bird has the sense to fight for her young. If a mama bird sees you going towards her nest, she will swoop down on you and try to peck your eyes out. If a bird can see danger approaching her chicks, why won't Christian parents bother to look? Don't tell me that animals show more responsibility for the gift that God has provided them than human beings do.

Demons possess children. Hollywood has made millions of dollars off childhood possession stories. They've even produced movies about children's toys or dolls being possessed. *Child's Play* and *Bride of Chucky* are prime examples. *Rosemary's Baby* is another good example of devil possession. Even our Holy Bible in Mathew 15:22-28, Mathew 17:14-18, and Mark 9:14-29 tells of demons possessing people. All these things are real, and parents had better wake up before it's too late to save their children.

Oh, No! Not My Little Angel

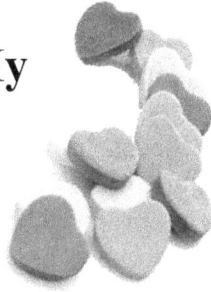

S ome parents refuse to spank or use other forms of discipline when their child has misbehaved or acted out of order. (Proverbs 19:18) The wicked and evil people of this world have made it unlawful to discipline children in private or public. They teach children to call 911 if a parent spanks them. These parents will not allow any person to speak a word of correction to their children. They, as well as their children, are out of control and on a path that leads to destruction. These types of parents (Christian and non-Christian) don't want to be disciplined and are in rebellion against God. (Romans 13:1-3, 2 Timothy 3:1-5)

What they don't realize is that if they don't do it themselves or if they won't allow someone else to chastise their children, Satan wins. If a child doesn't learn to submit to the authority of man whom he can see, how in the world will he ever be able to submit to the authority of God—who is a spirit and cannot be seen? (John 4:24)

Discipline your child while there is still hope.

There are three good reasons to do this. One, it keeps him from growing up thinking that the world revolves around him. Two, it keeps him from thinking that he's omnipotent and that nobody will ever challenge or correct his behavior. Three, it keeps him from thinking that he's better than everyone else—believing that his "stuff don't stink."

The prophet Samuel received a chastising hand from God because he didn't discipline his sons. (Samuel 2:12-17) Some parents say, "My child is a good child and would never do a thing like that." They seriously underestimate what a child is capable of doing. As for the Christian parents, they project their own goodness on the child. They fail to realize that the child is not saved yet and is still living under the curse of sin. The parents accepted Jesus as their Savior. When the child comes of age and knowledge, he has the opportunity to do so, too.

Preachers' kids, for example, are always getting picked on. People point the finger and say that they're the worst-behaved children around. They say that preachers' kids are the ones who get into trouble first. They expect the child to be as holy as the preacher. In reality, the child and the parent have two separate souls.

The Christian parent is the one who has to keep his child under a watchful eye and ask the Lord for protection. They can't just say, "My child knows better than to do anything to embarrass me. He knows that I'm a Christian. I set a good example of Christian behavior in front of him. My child's perfect because I'm perfect." Satan has deceived that parent into believing a big lie. He's hoodwinked both saved and unsaved parents into believing their children need no discipline, guidance, or correction. The truth is that little Johnny or Suzy needs way more than just a five minute timeout.

Tattoo My Name

Some people tattoo names and images on their skin. They think it's cute or hip. They want to keep in fashion with the world. Hitler's hatred was so great that he put tattoos on the Jews and sent them to death camps and gas chambers. Let's not forget that he sent some Christians there, too. Who do you think placed hatred for his fellow man in Hitler's heart? Hatred only comes from the devil. The devil says to put ink on your skin and mess yourself up so God can be mad at you. He says you aren't good enough the way you were born. "Go ahead and make your own designs on your skin because God didn't know what He was doing when He made you," he says.

People should always listen to God instead of Satan. God said that man was made in his image. (Genesis 1:26-27) Do you think our Holy Father has ink drawings all over and looks like a circus freak? I hope your answer is no, because He is the God of all creation. He is light, holiness, and righteousness. In Him, there is no darkness or sin.

Sin destroys everything in its path. It leads to eternal damnation. Tattooing yourself is a worldly tradition. It is neither godly nor biblical. We haven't been commanded by God to put marks or artistic designs on our bodies. Our bodies are the temples of the Holy Ghost. (Ephesians 2:19-22) Tattooing is a tool of the devil that prepares you to receive his mark of the beast. (Revelation 14:9-12) God marks His children, and the Devil marks his, too. The Lord God writes His children's names on the palm of His hand. Those names will never die or be forgotten. (Isaiah 49:14-16)

People tattoo their children's names on their bodies and say they will never forget them. They think the names will last forever. When death comes, these names go to the grave and rot with that person. They are dead and forgotten. A person who does not accept Jesus Christ as his Lord and Savior is already dead in trespasses and sin. Jesus is the way, the truth, and the life. Tattooing your children's names or anything else on your body is not going to help that child one bit. Christians who get tattoos or allow their children to get tattoos—even those fake ones that you wet with water and apply to the skin—are on a slippery slope. They're about to fall into the devil's trap. They could lose their very souls.

It's time to get wisdom and understanding of God's ways so your name will be written in the Book of Life. Bring your children to God so He will bless them. Let the Lord tattoo their names on the palm of His hands—where it counts. Let the Lord God put His mark on you and your children instead of some man with disease-laden ink. Don't let Satan fool you into believing that all tattoo needles are clean or deceive you into going to a Christian tattoo artist. Those artists are in error and rebellion against the Word of God.

Tattoo marks don't glorify your body, which belongs to God. The tattoo artist is just a man putting ink on your flesh. He's not the Lord God who marks and seals

52

you for eternity. Man's mark can be removed with a laser instrument. God's mark can never be removed. (Genesis 4:13-15) If you don't have God's mark, you're game for the devil's "666" mark. (Revelation 14:9-11) Don't think that if you have even a tiny tattoo, the angels who come to destroy can't find you. They know what God's mark looks like. Anything that's not of God is of the devil. Get ready for judgment and destruction. (Revelation 16:1-2) The fire of God is hot and will burn you and your tattoo designs up.

Parents—please come to Jesus, and bring your children, too. (2 Peter 3:8-10) Let Him love and comfort you. Don't be ignorant of His ways. Don't let Satan fool you anymore. Jesus is waiting, and He is able to take care of you.

Who Will Take The Children?

Adam and Eve were the first child murderers. When they disobeyed, death was released into the world. Not only did they die, but their future children died, too. When they opened the door to death, all creation began to die. They brought children into a fallen and decaying world. Jesus Christ came to redeem the world. He brought salvation and life back to us. If parents who aren't saved don't get right with God, they and their children will be destroyed.

God is getting ready to make a new Heaven and a new Earth. (Revelation 21:1) Only those who are saved, baptized, washed in the blood of the Lamb, and filled with the Holy Ghost will live in this new Heaven and Earth. Death and the soul that sins will never enter the Pearly Gates. They'll go to the lake of fire which burns forever. Mankind was created for eternity. There's no doubt about it—the soul will spend eternity somewhere. Why not take the precious gift of eternal life that Jesus has to offer you? Why not give your children a chance to live?

Sugar & HONEY

ABOUT THE AUTHOR

Sugar & Honey

Vanessa M. White is an aspiring writer. She is a retired Correctional Counselor with experience working in Jails and Prisons. By election of God she has been called and chosen to the Missionary/ Deaconess field. She has a great love and compassion for children. And want them to grow up in the knowledge and love of Jesus Christ.

I can be contacted at: white7475@centurylink.net

www.ingramcontent.com/pod-product-compliance
Lightning Source LLC
Chambersburg PA
CBHW071431040426
42445CB00012BA/1344